George McClellan

Union General

Colonial Leaders

Lord Baltimore
English Politician and Colonist

Benjamin Banneker
American Mathematician and Astronomer

Sir William Berkeley
Governor of Virginia

William Bradford
Governor of Plymouth Colony

Jonathan Edwards
Colonial Religious Leader

Benjamin Franklin
American Statesman, Scientist, and Writer

Anne Hutchinson
Religious Leader

Cotton Mather
Author, Clergyman, and Scholar

Increase Mather
Clergyman and Scholar

James Oglethorpe
Humanitarian and Soldier

William Penn
Founder of Democracy

Sir Walter Raleigh
English Explorer and Author

Caesar Rodney
American Patriot

John Smith
English Explorer and Colonist

Miles Standish
Plymouth Colony Leader

Peter Stuyvesant
Dutch Military Leader

George Whitefield
Clergyman and Scholar

Roger Williams
Founder of Rhode Island

John Winthrop
Politician and Statesman

John Peter Zenger
Free Press Advocate

Revolutionary War Leaders

John Adams
Second U.S. President

Samuel Adams
Patriot

Ethan Allen
Revolutionary Hero

Benedict Arnold
Traitor to the Cause

John Burgoyne
British General

George Rogers Clark
American General

Lord Cornwallis
British General

Thomas Gage
British General

King George III
English Monarch

Nathanael Greene
Military Leader

Nathan Hale
Revolutionary Hero

Alexander Hamilton
First U.S. Secretary of the Treasury

John Hancock
President of the Continental Congress

Patrick Henry
American Statesman and Speaker

William Howe
British General

John Jay
First Chief Justice of the Supreme Court

Thomas Jefferson
Author of the Declaration of Independence

John Paul Jones
Father of the U.S. Navy

Thaddeus Kosciuszko
Polish General and Patriot

Lafayette
French Freedom Fighter

James Madison
Father of the Constitution

Francis Marion
The Swamp Fox

James Monroe
American Statesman

Thomas Paine
Political Writer

Molly Pitcher
Heroine

Paul Revere
American Patriot

Betsy Ross
American Patriot

Baron Von Steuben
American General

George Washington
First U.S. President

Anthony Wayne
American General

Famous Figures of the Civil War Era

John Brown
Abolitionist

Jefferson Davis
Confederate President

Frederick Douglass
Abolitionist and Author

Stephen A. Douglas
Champion of the Union

David Farragut
Union Admiral

Ulysses S. Grant
Military Leader and President

Stonewall Jackson
Confederate General

Joseph E. Johnston
Confederate General

Robert E. Lee
Confederate General

Abraham Lincoln
Civil War President

George Gordon Meade
Union General

George McClellan
Union General

William Henry Seward
Senator and Statesman

Philip Sheridan
Union General

William Sherman
Union General

Edwin Stanton
Secretary of War

Harriet Beecher Stowe
Author of Uncle Tom's Cabin

James Ewell Brown Stuart
Confederate General

Sojourner Truth
Abolitionist, Suffragist, and Preacher

Harriet Tubman
Leader of the Underground Railroad

Famous Figures of the Civil War Era

George McClellan

Union General

Brent Kelley

Arthur M. Schlesinger, jr.
Senior Consulting Editor

Chelsea House Publishers

Philadelphia

CHELSEA HOUSE PUBLISHERS
Editor-in-Chief Sally Cheney
Director of Production Kim Shinners
Production Manager Pamela Loos
Art Director Sara Davis
Production Editor Diann Grasse

Staff for *GEORGE McCLELLAN*
Editor Sally Cheney
Associate Art Director Takeshi Takahashi
Series Design Keith Trego
Layout by D&G Limited, LLC

The Chelsea House World Wide Web address is
http://www.chelseahouse.com

First Printing
1 3 5 7 9 8 6 4 2

Library of Congress Cataloging-in-Publication Data

Kelley, Brent P.
    George McClellan / Brent Kelley.
        p. cm. — (Famous figures of the Civil War era)
    Includes bibliographical references and index.
    ISBN 0-7910-6404-2 (alk. paper) — ISBN 0-7910-6405-0 (pbk. :
    alk. paper)
      1. McClellan, George Brinton, 1826-1885—Juvenile literature.
    2. Generals—United States—Biography—Juvenile literature.
    3. United States. Army—Biography—Juvenile literature. 4. United
    States—History—Civil War, 1861-1865—Campaigns—Juvenile
    literature. [1. McClellan, George Brinton, 1826-1885. 2. Generals.
    3. United States—History—Civil War, 1861-1865] I. Title. II. Series.

    E467.1.M2 K45 2001
    973.7'41'092—dc21
    [B]   2001028763

Publisher's Note: In Colonial, Revolutionary War, and Civil War Era America, there were no standard rules for spelling, punctuation, capitalization, or grammar. Some of the quotations that appear in the Colonial Leaders, Revolutionary War Leaders, and Famous Figures of the Civil War Era series come from original documents and letters written during this time in history. Original quotations reflect writing inconsistencies of the period.

Contents

George McClellan's father kept a stable of trotting horses as a hobby. George's fondness for horses would play a part in his future as a cavalry officer.

The Doctor's Son

George Brinton McClellan was born on December 3, 1826. He was the second son and third child of Dr. George McClellan and Elizabeth Steinmetz Brinton McClellan of Philadelphia, Pennsylvania. The McClellans eventually had two more children, another son and another daughter. The children in the order of their birth were Frederica, John, George, Arthur, and Mary. Nothing indicated that one day little George would grow up to be the commander in chief of all the Northern armies during the Civil War.

George's father had a surgical practice in Philadelphia and specialized in **ophthalmology**.

Dr. McClellan was an energetic, hardworking man who, in addition to his practice, founded the Jefferson Medical College and served as the head of its faculty for a number of years. He also edited a medical journal, wrote a great deal on surgery and the practice of ophthalmology, and owned a stable of trotting horses. The horses were his hobby, and he devoted most of his spare time to them. George was particularly fond of them, too, and this fondness for them helped him become the fine cavalry officer he would be later in his life.

Doctor's were not wealthy in those days. It was a highly respected profession, but not one that brought in large amounts of money. The McClellan family had enough money to live comfortably, but they were not wealthy. Also, Dr. McClellan had inherited considerable debts from his father, and George's older brother, John, wanted to attend medical school, which was expensive. Because of all of this, an expensive higher education did not seem to be available to young George and his younger brother, Arthur.

George's mother, however, was a woman of culture and refinement. She insisted that her children, at least when they were still young, were given the best education that was available in Philadelphia.

When George was five years old he began his education, attending what was called an infant school. He spent two years there and learned reading, writing, mathematics, and languages. George was then enrolled in a private school headed by Sears Cook Walker, a Harvard graduate who later became an important man with the United States Naval Observatory and the Coast Survey. George studied under Mr. Walker until he was 10 years old.

For the next two years he studied with a German tutor named Mr. Schiffer, whom George later described as "a magnificent classical scholar & an excellent teacher." He went on to write that Mr. Schiffer required them to carry on their conversations in Latin and French. This would seem to be a challenging task for a young man not yet in his teens, but George was very intelligent and excelled at it. "At an early age I became a good scholar in the classics," he wrote later.

Young George was especially fond of his sister, Frederica, the oldest of the McClellan children. When he was a student at West Point and throughout his life he wrote many letters to her. She kept all of his letters, and he kept the ones from her. She, too, was very fond of her brother and much of what we know about his childhood, other than his schooling, comes from her. Both George and Frederica wrote of visits to their grandparents' home in Woodstock, Connecticut, trips that George really didn't like because he considered himself to be a Southerner and couldn't relate to some of the cultural differences of the Northerners.

Frederica wrote that George was "the brightest, merriest, most unselfish of boys," and said that he was "fond of books & study—& also of fun & frolic, & always the 'soul of honor.'"

In 1838, when he was not quite 12 years old, George's time with Mr. Schiffer was over, and he was enrolled in a preparatory academy for the University of Pennsylvania. This was run by the Reverend Samuel W. Crawford, a strict disciplinarian, as well as a highly respected scholar.

While at the preparatory school, when he was 13 years old he was wrongly accused of breaking some rules. The punishment for this was supposed to be a whipping with a rattan switch. Many years later, George recalled, "My father had told me not to permit myself to be whipped." When Reverend Crawford approached him with the switch, George "met him with a kick & went out of the school."

Dr. McClellan intervened on his son's behalf, peace was made with Reverend Crawford, and George was readmitted to the school. He said he "never had any more trouble with the rattan."

Whippings or spank-
ings of disobedient
or unruly students were
common in schools in the
1800s. In many cases,
these were done with
whips made of rattan.

Rattan is a kind of palm
that grows in India and
Africa. The dried stems
make a tough, stringy
material that can be made
into chair seats, but they
are also used to make
canes and switches. These
are very strong and
unlikely to break as a small
branch or twig from an
American tree may do.
Also, the rattan switches
sting more than switches
made from other materials.

George spent two years at the preparatory school under Reverend Crawford, and when he was 14 he entered the University of Pennsylvania. He had reluctantly decided he would become a lawyer because the cost of medical school was too great for his father.

At that time, George was not considering a military career. There was no strong military background in the McClellan family. George's great-grandfather, Samuel McClellan of Woodstock, Connecticut, served in the militia in the French and Indian War before the Revolutionary War and he remained in the militia through the Revolution. Although he saw no active duty, he was promoted to the rank of

George decided to attend the United States Military Academy at West Point. Many Civil War leaders, such as those from the North shown here, also attended West Point.

brigadier general in 1779. But Samuel's sons were educators, not military men, and both George's father and uncle were doctors.

Then after two years at the university, George began thinking about a military career and the possibility of going to the United States Military Academy in West Point, New York. He considered the potential challenge of this compared to what he considered the drudgery of a career as a lawyer and decided that a military career would be much more satisfying.

He talked it over with his father and was told to apply with his blessings. In late 1841, even though he was just 14 years old, he applied for admission to the United States Military Academy.

He waited for word of his acceptance, but it didn't come. Dr. McClellan took action. He wrote a letter to Secretary of War John C. Spencer saying, "The youth has nearly completed his classical education at the University and desires to go through the West Point school for the serious purpose of devoting his life to the service of the Army of the U. States." He asked the secretary to speak with President John Tyler on his son's behalf. It is not known whether President Tyler actually did anything to hasten the processing of George's application, but it was not long after that that his acceptance came.

In the summer of 1842, at age fifteen and a half, he was off to West Point to begin his military education.

Thomas "Stonewall" Jackson was George's classmate at West Point. Jackson would later become a Confederate general. He was accidentally shot by his own men at the Battle of Chancellorsville and died from his wounds.

Military Life at West Point

The years at West Point did not begin well for Conditional Cadet George McClellan. It was the first time he had been away from his family, and he was terribly homesick. This can be blamed, at least in part, on the fact that he was the youngest person at the Academy.

Also, the shoes that he was issued were too tight and his feet hurt, but after a short time he was given new shoes in the correct size, which lifted his spirits.

After an introductory period at the academy, the young men were given physical examinations. Thirty of those hoping to be accepted did not pass these physicals, but young George did. Next there was an entrance examination that he also passed easily. It was not a difficult test, but a few cadets with a poor education could not pass the test.

There was one more potential threat to his acceptance at West Point. The minimum age for entrance to the academy was 16. George missed this by six months, but the authorities waived this requirement in his case and he became a member of the class of 1846.

His first two months at West Point in 1842 were spent in summer encampment, where the cadets were taught the fundamentals of soldiering. This included the proper uniform, the use of the musket and bayonet, and the basic marching drills. The entire Corps of Cadets lived in tents, as they would do in a military campaign.

George didn't complain much about life at West Point. Most of the cadets, including George, didn't like the food and what always seemed to be day-old bread. Superintendent

Richard Delafield allowed them ample time for recreation and visits from friends and family, which pleased George.

By the end of the two months he felt at home as a cadet at the academy and wore his uniform with pride. He wrote to his mother that he "was becoming as tough as a pine log."

Classes finally began in September. The days were 12 hours long–2 or 3 hours of drill and 9 or 10 hours of studies in the classroom. That first year, only two subjects were taught: mathematics, which included algebra, trigonometry, and geometry; and French.

The subjects were no problem for George, who had received an excellent early education. At the mid-year examinations in January 1843, George ranked first in mathematics, but only eighth in French, a language he studied while in school in Philadelphia. He felt he already knew it and therefore did not study properly.

But for many cadets, the courses at the academy were more than they could handle; 51 of the 134 first-year cadets failed and had to leave the academy. One–Thomas J. Jackson of Virginia, who later would be called "Stonewall" Jackson–had a very difficult time, but made it through. At the end of the year George was third in "order of general merit." Thomas Jackson made it through in 51st place of the 83 survivors.

Even though George did well in his first year, he had poor study habits and only worked when he had to. He wrote to his brother John, "I never studied at all at home, now I do study a little (not much I must confess)."

The second year of school saw more mathematics (more geometry, plus calculus and surveying), more French, English composition and grammar, and drawing. The drawing course was meant to prepare the cadets for the military and civil engineering courses that would follow.

George described drawing as "hard work" and it was the first subject that he found to be difficult. After the year he ranked third overall in his class, but 18th in drawing.

In his third year there was more drawing, as well as chemistry and natural and experimental philosophy, which included mechanics, **acoustics**, optics, and astronomy. His drawing did not improve; he fell to 23rd in drawing and because of this dropped to 4th place in his class.

The summer encampments continued. Cadets learned field maneuvers, artillery, entrenching, pontoon bridging, fortification, and riding, but were not taught cavalry strategy. This was taught in the second and fourth summers. The cadets were given two months off in the third summer. This break was viewed with great anticipation. They could go home.

George was well liked by students and faculty alike. Erasmus Keyes, the artillery instructor,

The rules at West Point were tough and strictly enforced. Breaking the rules meant demerits and the number differed according to the infraction.

Demerits were given out for sloppiness of dress, uncleanness, poorly maintained equipment, tardiness, improper preparation, and several other things. Drunkenness was a serious offense that could lead to a court martial and dismissal.

wrote that "a pleasanter pupil was never called to the blackboard," and fellow cadet Dabney Maury of Virginia wrote that George had "every evidence of gentle nature and high culture . . ."

There were times when George believed that he was the victim of faculty unfairness. When he finished second in both chemistry and natural philosophy in the January 1854 exams, he complained in a letter to his mother that he had done better than the student above him. He felt that to be recognized he would "have to get a much better mark" than the other student. He wrote, "toiling up hill is not what it is cracked up to be!"

He came to feel that life was unfair. When he learned of the death of Frederica's three-year-old daughter, he wrote his sister, "A long struggle in this world is all that life consists of." He was trying to comfort her, but he spoke of the unhappiness that he thought awaited those who grew to maturity.

Fourth year classes included infantry and artillery tactics, **mineralogy** and geology, ethics

The Battle of Palo Alto in May 1846, took place before President Polk signed a formal declaration of war with Mexico. The Mexican-American War would continue through 1847. At the end of the war, the Treaty of Guadalupe Hidalgo set the southern boundary of Texas and gave New Mexico and California to the United States.

(which covered the study of constitutional and international law, logic, and philosophy), and

"Old Rough and Ready" Zachary Taylor fought in the Mexican-American War.

"Military and Civil Engineering and the Science of War." This latter subject was George's favorite, and he was first in his class in this course.

At the end of the fourth year, George was president of the Dialectic Society, a club that was made up of the best of the academy's upper classmen. The group met once a week to discuss important issues in society. Membership was by invitation only. As the president, George gave the valedictory address (a speech made to the graduating class) and felt that he should be number one in his class, based on his overall accomplishments of the previous four years.

But Charles S. Stewart was named number one. George did not accept this easily. He wrote to his family, "I must confess that I have malice enough to want to show them that if I did not graduate head of my class, I can nevertheless do something."

During his fourth year at West Point, the big news was the dispute over the border between Texas and Mexico. The fourth year cadets, and especially George, were excited over the news of General Zachary Taylor's exploits and President James Polk's message of war. George wrote Frederica, "Hip! Hip! Hurrah! War at last sure enough! Aint it glorious! . . . Well, it appears that our wishes have at last been gratified & we shall soon have the intense satisfaction of fighting . . ."

On July 1, 1846, George received his commission as a **brevet** second lieutenant in the Corps of Engineers. He went home to Philadelphia on leave, but after a few days he was ordered back to West Point for duty in the new Company of Engineer Soldiers, an elite company. He wrote Frederica that this was "all that I could hope, ask, or expect; it is exactly what I desired." He was third in command behind Captain Alexander T. Swift and first lieutenant G. W. Smith, one of George's instructors at West Point and one of his best friends.

The officers trained the recruits and in September 1846, they sailed for the mouth of the Rio Grande River to fight in the Mexican-American

They went on to Puebla and took that city. While there, word came that George's father had died. Dr. McClellan was only 50 years old. George was also told that his father had left many debts. George accepted responsibility for the debts and vowed that they would all be paid off. He was able to do this within a few years by selling a land grant given to him for his participation in the Mexican-American War.

George fought in the Battles of Contreras and Churubusco. He was promoted to first lieutenant "for gallant and meritorious conduct."

U.S. troops reached Mexico City, and on September 14, General Santa Anna, whose troops were defending the city, fled. The United States forces moved in and occupied the Mexican capital for nine months before an armistice could be worked out and a peace treaty was official.

George was just 20 years old at the end of the Mexican-American War. He returned to duty at West Point. Within a short time he was bored with his life there and even stopped keeping a

Captain Randolph Marcy and George went on government expeditions and became life-long friends. Marcy eventually became George's father-in-law.

journal on a regular basis, making entries only once in a while. As always, he longed for action.

On April 1, 1852, he was ordered to Fort Smith, Arkansas, to take part in an expedition to find the sources of the Red River. He was second in command to Captain Randolph Marcy, who would become a lifelong friend.

Their expedition was a success, and in October 1852 George was assigned the task of surveying the rivers and harbors along the Texas coast. George did an excellent job.

His next assignment, in 1853, was to help survey a route from St. Paul, Minnesota, to Puget Sound in Washington State for a possible transcontinental railroad. This was the first time that he did not do an outstanding job. His portion of the survey was to find a pass through the Cascade Mountains in Washington that would be satisfactory for railroad tracks. He concluded that there were no suitable passes, even though he had only examined two. The Native Americans of the area told him those were the only choices and he believed them rather than checking on his own. There were actually three other passes, all of which were eventually used for passageways.

He returned to the East Coast. There he met Captain Marcy's wife, who had left the frontier

George depended on information supplied by Native Americans while he was surveying a route from Minnesota to Washington State.

and returned to Washington. It was then that George met 18-year-old Mary Ellen "Nell" Marcy. George asked Mrs. Marcy for permission to court Mary Ellen. Mrs. Marcy was fond of George and gave him permission. After a short courtship, George proposed marriage in June of 1854. Nell turned him down.

George was unhappy about this, but fortunately he had an assignment almost immediately. That same month he sailed on the

Columbia, sent to the Dominican Republic by Secretary of War Jefferson Davis to select and survey an anchorage that might be used by the Navy. Davis wanted a site in the Caribbean Sea to balance Britain's stronghold in Jamaica.

The future president of the Confederate States of America admired the young McClellan and thought he would accomplish great things. When George returned from the Dominican Republic Davis assigned him the task of investigating the country's railroads, a challenging undertaking that would benefit him in just a few years.

He was made a captain and was a member of the new First Cavalry. This group was sent to Texas on March 3, 1855, to oversee the territorial gains from the Mexican peace treaty. While in Texas, he was able to renew his friendship with Randolph Marcy.

At about the same time, Jefferson Davis requested permission from President Franklin Pierce to send a commission to Europe to study the latest military developments and to observe firsthand the war in the Crimea. The president approved, and the commissioners left in April 1855. The two senior members of the commission were Majors Richard Delafield and Alfred Mordecai, both veteran officers. For the third member, Davis selected George McClellan, still not 30 years old. These men inspected the armies of Austria, Prussia, France, and Britain.

While in Europe, George observed the different types of saddles used by the cavalries there. They were different from the U.S. Cavalry saddles and much more practical. Borrowing from the Hungarian and Prussian saddles, with a little bit from others, he designed a new saddle, called the McClellan saddle, that was used by the U. S. Cavalry until that branch of the Army was disbanded.

George made his report of the commission's findings in Europe, but as he was doing so he complained to friends that he was unhappy with what he was doing. He needed more challenging work.

On November 26, 1857, he wrote of his intentions to resign his commission, effective

January 15, 1857. As he put it to Randolph Marcy, "I fancy you were rather surprised at my sudden departure from my old paths—I was rather so myself."

There were a few civilian jobs available, but nothing was interesting to him. His friend, G. W. Smith, now a civil engineer, introduced him to Abram S. Hewitt, who in turn introduced him to Samuel L. M. Barlow, a lawyer who was the same age as George. They became close friends and through Barlow's connections George found an executive job at the Illinois Central Railroad.

George did his new job well and within a year he was made vice president with a salary of $5,000 a year, a significant amount of money at the time. But he was lonely. He wrote to Nell, whom he now called Ellen, "Can't you find among your acquaintances some quiet young woman . . . who can sew on buttons, look happy when I come home . . ." Ellen did not answer.

The job with the railroad soon became boring. George wrote to friends that he may have

Ambrose Burnside, a year behind George at West Point, left the Army in 1853 to manufacture carbines, but the Panic of 1857 caused his bankruptcy. He wrote George seeking a job with the Illinois Central, and George hired him as a cashier for the railroad. George also offered to let him share his house in Chicago, and they became great friends.

Like George, Burnside returned to the military and became a general in the Army of the Potomac. He wore his hair growing down the side his face and that hair came to be known as "sideburns."

made a mistake to leave the military. He even considered becoming a **soldier of fortune** to fight in the many civil upheavals that were taking place in Latin America.

But then the Panic of 1857 struck. This was a severe financial crisis that drove many businesses to bankruptcy. The Illinois Central was in trouble, and the president of the company in New York ordered services altered and wages cut. In October 1857, George said that the workers were making less than a dollar a day and that he would not allow their wages to be lowered. He also said that he would not accept any more salary until the crisis ended.

The president of the Illinois Central, William H. Osborn, and George did not agree on several things. George was named to head the recovery of the railroad, but was frequently at odds with Osborn. He considered quitting to rejoin the army.

This seemed to be a good time to join the army again. In Utah there was a war between the Mormons and the U.S. government over who would govern the state. His friend Marcy was sent there and George tried to re-enlist as a colonel. But the Mormon War ended without any bloodshed and the need for officers was no longer there, so he stayed with the railroad.

Still, he did not like the life he was leading. He had a personal library of hundreds of books on war and history and he studied them. He had written to Ellen at one point, "–it is war on a large scale that interests me . . ."

And although he disliked business, he was good at it. He doubled the Illinois Central's reach. Originally running from Chicago in the north to Cairo, Illinois, in the south, he made contracts with riverboats to haul goods all the way from Cairo to New Orleans. He planned tracks to cover that distance, but the Civil War stopped the plan. It was eventually accomplished after the war, just as George had designed it.

Ellen finally began answering his letters. She was still single, although she had received many proposals of marriage from men of all ages. Actually, both of her parents still wanted her to marry George.

In 1859, Captain Marcy was assigned to St. Paul, Minnesota, and he took his family. On the way they passed through Chicago, and George invited them to stay with him in his home for a few days. When it came time for them to take the train to St. Paul, George decided to accompany them. On the trip he proposed to Ellen again and this time she accepted.

They were married on May 22, 1860, at the Calvary Church in New York. George was 33 and Ellen was 25. Two weeks after the wedding George wrote his mother, "I believe I am the

**George married Mary Ellen "Nell"
Marcy on May 22, 1860. George and Nell
had written to each other for years
before Nell accepted George's proposal
of marriage.**

happiest man that ever lived & am sure that I
have the dearest wife in all the world."

In late June 1860, Samuel Barlow offered
George a job restoring the Ohio and Mississippi

Union General Ambrose Burnside, shown here, and George were friends for many years both in the military and in civilian life.

Railroad, which ran from Cincinnati to St. Louis. The railroad went out of business in the Panic of 1857. At the time the offer came, George was having more problems with William Osborn, so

Shown here are Union soldiers ready for battle.

forces there. Shortly after, the *New York Herald* published a column praising him that was headed, "Gen. McClellan, the Napoleon of the Present War" and it was not long before other papers were referring to him as the "Napoleon of America" or "the Young Napoleon."

Because of this performance in Virginia he was made commander of the Union Army in the East, which came to be known as the Army of the Potomac. In a short time he had it organized into an efficient fighting force.

A little while later he was made general in chief of all the Union armies, but President Lincoln never felt that George acted quickly enough, which was borne out in future situations. In early 1862, Lincoln removed him as the general in chief, but he remained an Army commander. In addition to Lincoln's dislike, he was also intensely disliked by Secretary of War Edwin Stanton.

As the war escalated, George felt it imperative that the Union forces take Richmond, Virginia, and he devised what was to be called the Peninsular Campaign. He sailed with thousands of troops and arms to the James River at Yorktown to begin the march to Richmond.

He asked for more troops, but President Lincoln feared for the safety of Washington, D. C., and would not send all that George wanted. George began to feel that there was a conspiracy around him because he was denied what he thought he needed. As it was, he did not have enough manpower, he felt, to capture Yorktown and Gloucester.

So he did not attack. Southern General Joseph Johnston, in charge of the Confederate forces at Yorktown, was amazed that the city was spared. "No one but McClellan would have hesitated to attack," he wrote.

But the soldiers under his command believed in him. A member of General Joseph Hooker's troops wrote that the men "have every confidence in his ability." And he was confident in his abilities. He wrote to Ellen, "I do believe that I am . . . quietly preparing the way for a great success." Still, he did not attack.

By the time he was ready to lay siege to Yorktown, General Johnston had retreated, with his 56,000 men, to Williamsburg, 12 miles away.

Union troops under General Edwin Sumner engaged Johnston's army in Williamsburg, and the fighting could be heard by McClellan and his men. Instead of rushing to Williamsburg,

These Union soldiers were in charge of protecting George's position against Confederate assaults on Malvern Hill in Virginia.

George waited for a call for assistance from Sumner, which came too late for the Union to defeat the Confederates. When George's men arrived, Johnston had retreated again.

George did not like Sumner. He wrote to Ellen that Sumner "proved that he was even a greater fool than I had supposed . . ."

Pursuit of Johnston's forces could have been attempted, but there had been heavy rains for days and the road conditions were not suitable so Johnston escaped again.

For three weeks, George and his army made no progress. Rains had slowed them and he had been sick with his "Mexican disease," a bout with malarial fever. Lincoln was growing impatient. He told a newsman that he was unhappy with McClellan and was seriously considering replacing him.

But by late May, George had advanced to within six miles of Richmond. On May 31 and June 1, 1862, Johnston attacked at the Battle of Fair Oaks. Early in the fighting, the Confederate forces had the advantage, but the Union troops prevailed and the Southerners were driven back toward Richmond.

This battle was significant because General Johnston was wounded, and Confederate President Jefferson Davis replaced him with General Robert E. Lee.

George's Union army was straddled on each side of the Chickahominy River. Lee's forces were strengthened by the addition of the troops of George's old West Point classmate Joseph "Stonewall" Jackson. With stronger forces, Lee attacked McClellan's army in a series of battles called the Seven Days' Battle, so named because they were fought over the period of June 25 through July 1, 1862. It was a give-and-take series. The South took some and the North took some, but in the end George felt that he was seriously outnumbered, and he retreated to the James River. Richmond was not captured.

Finally help came. George's troops were joined by those of General John Pope, and George was put in charge of all of them. But before the two armies could join, General Lee attacked Pope's forces at the Second Battle of Bull Run on August 29 and 30, 1862. George was on his way to join Pope, but the Confederates won the battle and the South regained all of Virginia. The war was not going well for either the North or George at this point.

General Lee was feeling powerful because of his recent victory, so he decided to invade Union

General Robert E. Lee was a skilled military leader in the U.S. Army before the Civil War began. He left the U.S. Army and fought for the South during the war. Lee would eventually surrender to General Grant to end the war.

territory. For his first move, he sent Stonewall Jackson to capture Harpers Ferry, Maryland, which he did easily. A few days later George encountered Lee and his men at Antietam Creek, but delayed an attack until September 17. This allowed Jackson's men to rejoin Lee.

What may have been little more than a skirmish had McClellan acted quickly turned out to be one of the bloodiest battles of the Civil War. Both sides had heavy losses; the North suffered more than 12,000 killed and wounded and the South nearly that many. But Lee was repelled and was driven back into Virginia.

The victory was what President Lincoln had been waiting for. He took the opportunity to announce his Emancipation Proclamation, declaring slaves free in the Confederate states as of January 1, 1863.

Ellen was still in Cincinnati, where, on October 12, 1862, she gave birth to her first child, Mary, whom they always called "May." A few weeks later, George rented a house in Washington and sent for her and his daughter.

After the victory at Antietam, George again did not act quickly enough against Lee's army to satisfy Lincoln. He did not follow up this victory,

The bloodiest one-day battle of the Civil War took place at Antietam Creek in Maryland on September 17, 1862.

and it was the last straw for the president and Secretary Stanton. Lincoln said that he felt McClellan did not want to hurt the enemy and always moved too slowly. Also, Lincoln feared that George held political aspirations, since he was very popular among the Democrats. The president replaced him with one of George's best friends, General Ambrose Burnside.

George's removal from command was questioned by many. His friend, Fitz John Porter,

George McClellan's classmate at West Point, General Thomas "Stonewall" Jackson, was accidentally wounded by his own men at the Battle of Chancellorsville on May 2, 1863. His left arm had to be amputated and while surgery was being performed, General Robert E. Lee commented, "He has lost his left arm, but I have lost my right arm." Jackson died on May 10 from complications of the amputation combined with pneumonia.

The South won the Battle of Chancellorsville, defeating Northern troops led by General Joseph Hooker, but lost one of it greatest generals.

wrote in the *New York World,* "What can be the notion, what the justification, of relieving a successful general in the midst of a campaign . . . ?"

But Lee felt differently. Upon hearing the news that McClellan was taken out of action, he commented, "I fear they may continue to make these changes till they find some one whom I don't understand."

Burnside attacked Lee's forces at Fredericksburg, Virginia, on December 13, 1862, and it turned out to be one of the worst defeats the North suffered in the war. Burnside lost more than 12,000 men, killed or wounded, while the South's losses were less than half that. The defeat

He was asked to run for governor of Ohio in 1863, but declined. Instead, he moved back to New Jersey, where he entered politics on October 13, 1863. On that date, he came out in favor of Judge George W. Wood in the Pennsylvania **gubernatorial** race, but **incumbent** Governor Andrew G. Curtin won reelection.

He knew that this show of political activity meant he would never get another military assignment while Lincoln was president, so he considered resigning from the army. He was offered the job as president of the New Jersey Railroad at $5,000 a year, but the job did not come through. He decided not to tender his army resignation after all.

In 1864 the Ohio and Mississippi Railroad was sold and, because of his successful running of it a few years before, he was given a one-sixth share of the proceeds. This amounted to nearly $20,000.

On March 13, 1864, he wrote to his mother and did not say he was willing to run for the presidency, but insinuated that he would if asked. He said in the letter, "I know that all things will prove in the end to have been arranged for the best and am quite willing to accept what I cannot avoid."

The war was not going well and on August 22, 1864, President Lincoln was warned that it appeared that he would lose the upcoming election. Lincoln agreed.

One week later, on August 29, 1864, the Democratic convention began in Chicago. Although there was great sentiment favoring George as the party's nominee, George did not even attend the convention, instead staying at his home in New Jersey.

But George was chosen on the first ballot, despite the platform chosen by the Democrats' platform committee. This platform called for peace regardless of the cost, and George wanted a war victory. This alone made the campaign difficult, and it was made more so by the nomination of peace candidate George H. Pendleton of Ohio for vice president.

This political cartoon depicts George after his retreat from battle at Malvern Hill.

George refused the peace platform. He wrote to his friend and adviser Samuel Cox, "I could not have run on the platform . . . without violating all my antecedents–which I would not do for a thousand Presidencies." He considered reunion to be a vital part of any peace and he saw victory at war as the only way to gain reunion.

As bleak as things seemed to be for Lincoln a few days before, everything changed almost overnight. On September 1, 1864, General William Tecumseh Sherman took Atlanta. A short time before, Admiral David Farragut won a major battle at Mobile Bay. Then on September 10, General Philip Sheridan won decisively in the Shenandoah Valley of Virginia. All of these were popular victories and the citizens looked favorably on Lincoln as a result.

Perhaps things would have been different if George had campaigned, but he made only two public appearances before the election, and neither was in Pennsylvania, considered to be an important state for the Democrats.

In the meantime, Secretary Stanton was doing what he could for Lincoln. Allan Pinkerton, a spy and confidant used by George in the war, told George that Stanton believed that George and his friends were conspiring to assassinate Lincoln, and Pinkerton reported that Stanton was prepared to hang them if they did anything suspicious.

In October 1864, a few weeks before the presidential election, there were state and congressional elections held in Ohio, Pennsylvania, and Indiana, three states important to George's chances. All three went Republican. Still, a few days before the presidential election, George said he was confident of victory.

But he was wrong. In the popular vote, Lincoln received 55 percent of the votes to 45 percent for George. Lincoln received 212 electoral votes to only 21 for George, who carried only Kentucky, Missouri, and Delaware. What was most disheartening was the soldier vote; 78 percent went for Lincoln. It was considered not so much a defeat of George as it was a defeat of the peace platform.

He told his old friend Samuel Barlow that he was just as happy not to have the burdens of the presidency, but that he deplored the outcome for the country's sake.

George was still a young man; he turned 38 a few weeks after the election. A friend arranged for him to interview for the presidency of the Morris and Essex Railroad, but the

Secretary of War Edwin Stanton was a strong supporter of Lincoln throughout the war and during Lincoln's political campaigns.

board of directors turned him down because they feared that his defeat in the presidential election would hurt the railroad's chances of government contracts.

Money was not a problem. He received $5,000 a year from renting the home given to him in New York, and he had invested the $20,000 from the sale of the Ohio and Mississippi Railroad and received a handsome income from that. He discussed with Ellen what the future would be, and they decided to live in Europe for a while. They were there three and a half years.

The Europeans loved him. Ellen wrote her father, "The feeling for the General in England is enthusiastic–they look upon him as *the* American General." In Rome, George wrote to Samuel Barlow, ". . . all treat me as a gentleman. . . . Here we are the equals of the best . . . "

He was in Europe when he received word of Lincoln's assassination. He wrote that he was filled with "unmingled horror and regret."

Even though he was in Europe, George was still being considered by some to be a possible presidential candidate in 1868. But Ulysses S.

The McClellans spent much of 1865 in Rome, but with winter approaching they decided to move to Dresden, Germany, which they did in October. Mrs. Marcy and her younger daughter Fanny were with them, partially because Ellen was pregnant with their second child.

While in Dresden, on November 23, 1865, George Brinton McClellan Jr. was born. George, Sr., wrote his mother, " . . . he looks about him as wisely as a young owl and bids fair to be a good specimen." The family called him simply Max.

Grant was nominated by the Republican Party, and this ended any consideration of George. It was reasoned that George couldn't defeat the man who took Richmond, while he was the man who failed at the task. The McClellans returned to the United States to see Horatio Seymour be nominated by the Democratic Party.

George worked at engineering and railroad jobs for a few years, then in the spring of 1873 he began his own company: "George B. McClellan & Co., Consulting Engineers & Accountants." The company's prospectus said it represented "the interests of European investors in American Railroad Securities." He returned to Europe in October to introduce his company to bankers. He stayed in Europe for two years.

Upon his return to the United States in 1876 he got back into politics, campaigning for Democratic presidential candidate Samuel J. Tilden against the Republican Rutherford B. Hayes. Tilden won the popular vote, but Hayes won the electoral vote and was the new president.

With this renewed interest in politics, he won the New Jersey governor's race and served from 1878 to 1881. In his three-year term he accomplished a great deal without seeming to work too hard. Even though he went to Trenton, the capital, only on Tuesdays, he gave this as his reason for not running again—too much time in Trenton.

He visited Europe again in 1881 and later toured the Red River area with his father-in-law where they had explored years before.

In early October 1885, George had severe chest pains and was told by his doctor that he needed to rest. George felt better for a time, but

Union Civil War hero Ulysses S. Grant became the 18th president, serving from 1869 to 1877.

on October 28 the pain returned. At three o'clock in the morning on October 29 he died.

He was only 58 years old. His death was reported in newspapers around the country. His obituary in the *New York World* ended with "History will do him justice."

GLOSSARY

acoustics–structure that determines how sound can be transmitted.

armistice–a temporary peace.

brevet–a commission promoting an officer to a higher rank without a pay increase.

carbine–an automatic rifle.

dysentery–an intestinal disease with diarrhea.

gubernatorial–having to do with a governor.

incumbent–currently holding an office.

malaria–a disease transmitted by mosquitoes.

mineralogy–the science of minerals.

ophthalmology–the study of diseases of the eye.

pompous–acting important.

secede–withdraw from an organization.

soldier of fortune–a person who follows a military career wherever there is the possibility of money or adventure.

subordinate–lower in rank.

CHRONOLOGY

1826	Born in Philadelphia, Pennsylvania, on December 3.
1842	Entered United States Military Academy at West Point, New York.
1846	Graduated from West Point.
1847	Fought in the Mexican-American War.
1852	Began expedition to find sources of the Red River.
1853	Surveyed Cascade Mountains in Washington.
1855	Went to Europe as member of a commission to study the European military.
1857	Left military service on January 15; hired by Illinois Central Railroad.
1860	Married Mary Ellen Marcy on May 22; began work for Ohio and Mississippi Railroad.
1861	Rejoined Army as major general, later named general in chief of all Northern armies.
1862	Removed from his post as general in chief; defeated South at the Battle of Fair Oaks and at the Battle of Antietam.
1862	Relieved of duty in November; assigned to Trenton, New Jersey; daughter Mary born on October 12.
1864	Nominated for president by Democratic Party in August; lost election to Abraham Lincoln in November.
1865	Son George Brinton McClellan Jr., born on November 13; lived in Europe until 1868.

1873	Founded investment company, Geroge B. McClellan & Co., Consulting Engineers and Accountants.
1878	Governor of New Jersey until 1881.
1885	Died in Orange Mountain, New Jersey, on October 29.

CIVIL WAR TIME LINE ═══════

1860   Abraham Lincoln is elected president of the United States on November 6. During the next few months, Southern states begin to break away from the Union.

1861   On April 12, the Confederates attack Fort Sumter, South Carolina, and the Civil War begins. Union forces are defeated in Virginia at the First Battle of Bull Run (First Manassas) on July 21 and withdraw to Washington, D.C.

1862   Robert E. Lee is placed in command of the main Confederate army in Virginia in June. Lee defeats the Army of the Potomac at the Second Battle of Bull Run (Second Manassas) in Virginia on August 29–30. On September 17, Union general George B. McClellan turns back Lee's first invasion of the North at Antietam Creek near Sharpsburg, Maryland. It is the bloodiest day of the war.

1863   On January 1, President Lincoln issues the Emancipation Proclamation, freeing slaves in Southern states. Between May 1–6, Lee wins an important victory at Chancellorsville, but key Southern commander Thomas J. "Stonewall" Jackson dies from wounds. In June, Union forces hold the city of Vicksburg, Mississippi, under siege. The people of Vicksburg surrender on July 4. Lee's second invasion of the North during July 1–3 is decisively turned back at Gettysburg, Pennsylvania.

1864 General Grant is made supreme Union commander on March 9. Following a series of costly battles, on June 19 Grant successfully encircles Lee's troops in Petersburg, Virginia. A siege of the town lasts nearly a year.

Union general William Sherman captures Atlanta on September 2 and begins the "March to the Sea," a campaign of destruction across Georgia and South Carolina. On November 8, Abraham Lincoln wins reelection as president.

1865 On April 2, Petersburg, Virginia, falls to the Union. Lee attempts to reach Confederate forces in North Carolina but is gradually surrounded by Union troops. Lee surrenders to Grant on April 9 at Appomattox, Virginia, ending the war. Abraham Lincoln is assassinated by John Wilkes Booth on April 14.

FURTHER READING

Adler, David A. *A Picture Book of Robert E. Lee.* New York: Holiday House, 1998.

Copeland, Peter. *From Antietam to Gettysburg.* Mineola, NY: Dover, 1983.

Fritz, Jean. *Stonewall.* New York: Putnam, 1979.

Harness, Cheryl. *Abe Lincoln Goes to Washington, 1837-1865.* Washington: National Geographic Society, 1997.

Vandiver, Frank E. *1001 Things Everyone Should Know About the Civil War.* New York: Broadway Books.

PICTURE CREDITS

INDEX

Note: **Boldface** numbers indicate illustrations.

ABOUT THE AUTHOR

BRENT KELLEY is an equine veterinarian and writer. He is the author of many books on baseball history. Two books (written under the pen name Grant Kendall) tell about his experiences as a veterinarian. Brent has also written several books for Chelsea House. He is a columnist for *Thoroughbred Times*, a weekly horse racing and breeding publication, and also writes for *Bourbon Times*